Simply Rock

18 Rockin' Hits of the 1980s

Arranged by Dan Coates

Simply Rock 80s is a collection of some of the best rock songs from one of the most defining decades in pop music history. These songs have been carefully selected and arranged by Dan Coates for Easy Piano, making them accessible to pianists of all ages. Phrase markings, articulations, fingering and dynamics have been included to aid with interpretation, and a large print size makes the notation easy to read.

The 1980s was a time of new trends in the world of music. New technology, including synthesizers, electronic keyboards and drum machines, changed the sound of music and left an imprint on the recordings of the decade. Music television and music videos redefined the way audiences related to music; artists' personalities and appearance became increasingly important factors in their audience appeal. Michael Jackson, The Cars, Journey, Mike + The Mechanics—these were some of the artists that thrived with these changes. Songs from the decade range from intimate ballads like Journey's *Open Arms* to driving anthems like Survivor's *Eye of the Tiger*, and provide catchy melodies and dancing rhythms. For these reasons and more, rock music from the 1980s is exciting to explore.

After all, it is *Simply Rock 80s*!

Cover illustration by Sarah Lewis

Contents

At This Moment

Words and Music by Billy Vera
Arranged by Dan Coates

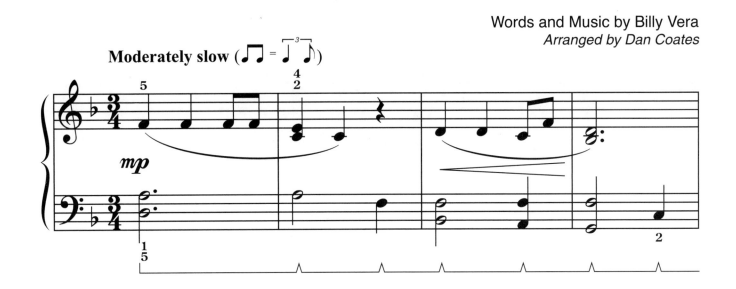

What did you think I would do at this
What did you think I would say at this

mo - ment, when you're stand - ing be - fore me with
mo - ment, when I'm faced with the know - ledge that

35
dar - lin', I love you?____ And you know

38
I'd nev - er hurt you.____ Oh,____

41
what do you think I would give at this

44
mo - ment? If you'd stay I'd sub - tract twen - ty

mf

Beat It

Written and Composed by Michael Jackson
Arranged by Dan Coates

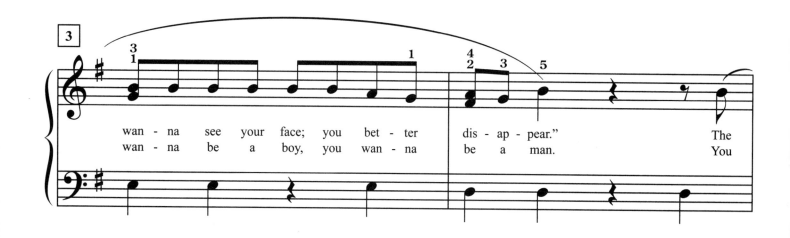

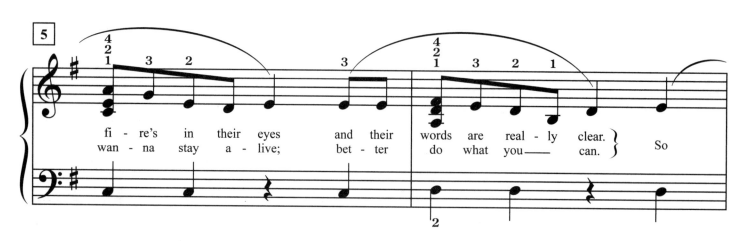

Billie Jean

Written and Composed by Michael Jackson
Arranged by Dan Coates

Steady rock beat

She was more like a beau - ty queen from a mov - ie scene.
For for - ty days and for for - ty nights law was on her side.

I said don't mind, but what do you mean I am the one
But who can stand when she's in de - mand, her schemes and plans,

claims that I   am the one,   but the kid is not my son.

She says I   am the one,   but the

kid is not my son.

mp

The Boys of Summer

Words and Music by
Don Henley and Mike Campbell
Arranged by Dan Coates

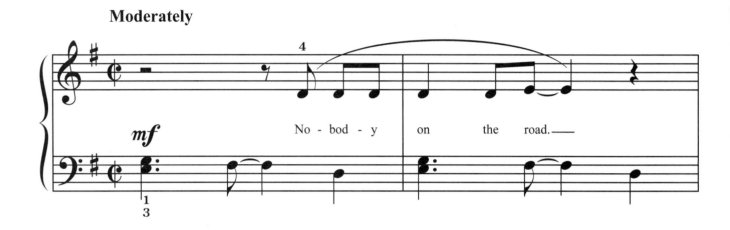

Broken Wings

Words and Music by Richard Page,
Steve George and John Lang
Arranged by Dan Coates

Medium fast rock

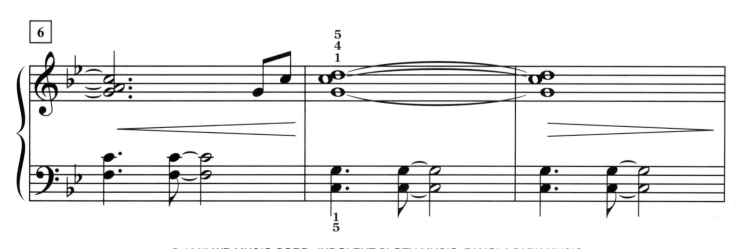

20

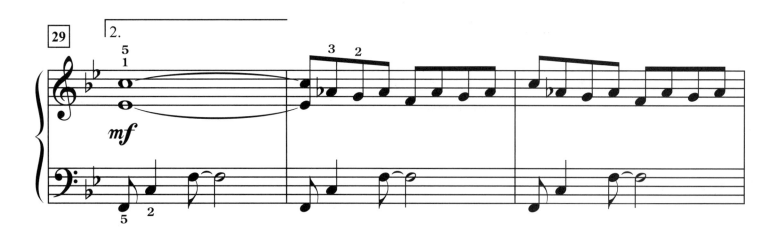

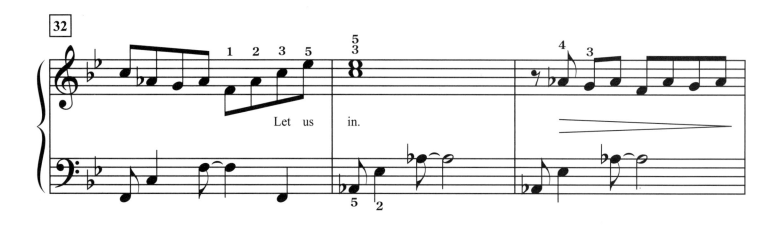

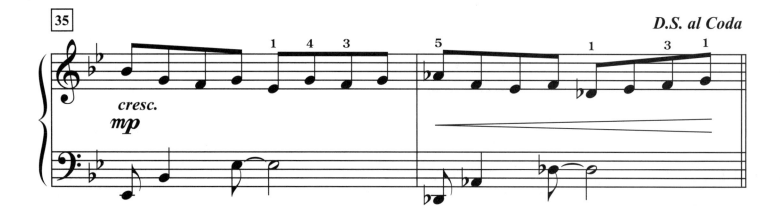

Don't You Know What the Night Can Do?

Words and Music by
Steve Winwood and Will Jennings
Arranged by Dan Coates

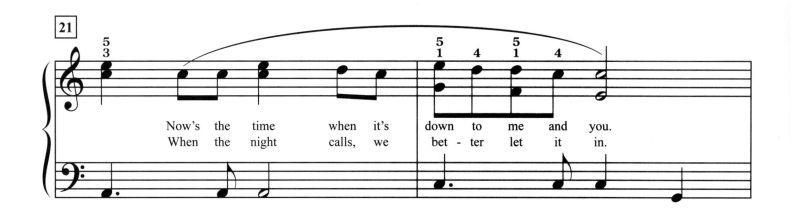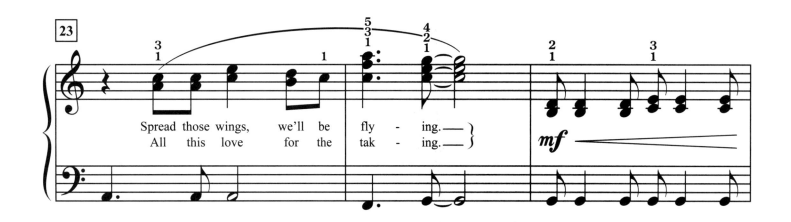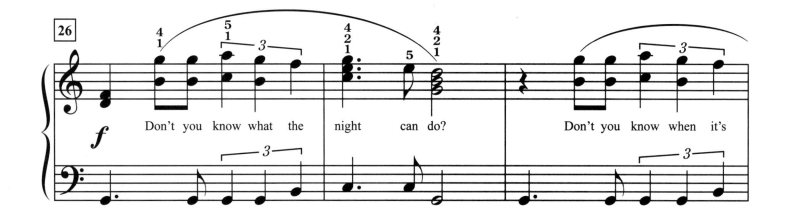

32 **2.** Won't you help me to let it through?

34 Don't you know what the night can do? Don't you *mf*

37 know what the night can do? Know what the night can do? Don't you

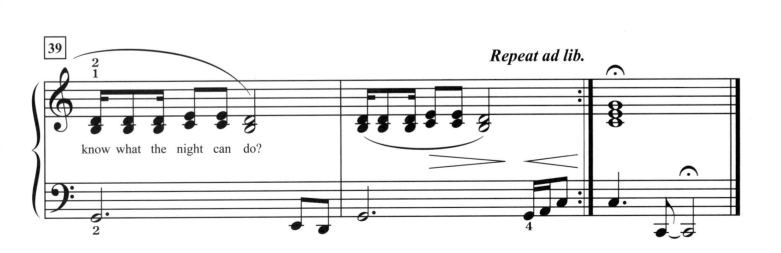

39 Repeat ad lib.

know what the night can do?

Drive

Words and Music by Ric Ocasek
Arranged by Dan Coates

Moderately

Who's gon - na tell you when
Who's gon - na hold you down

it's
when

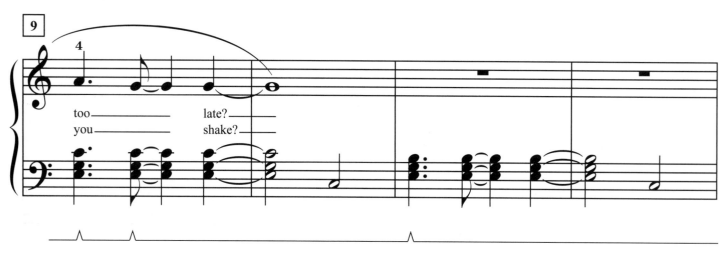

too late?
you shake?

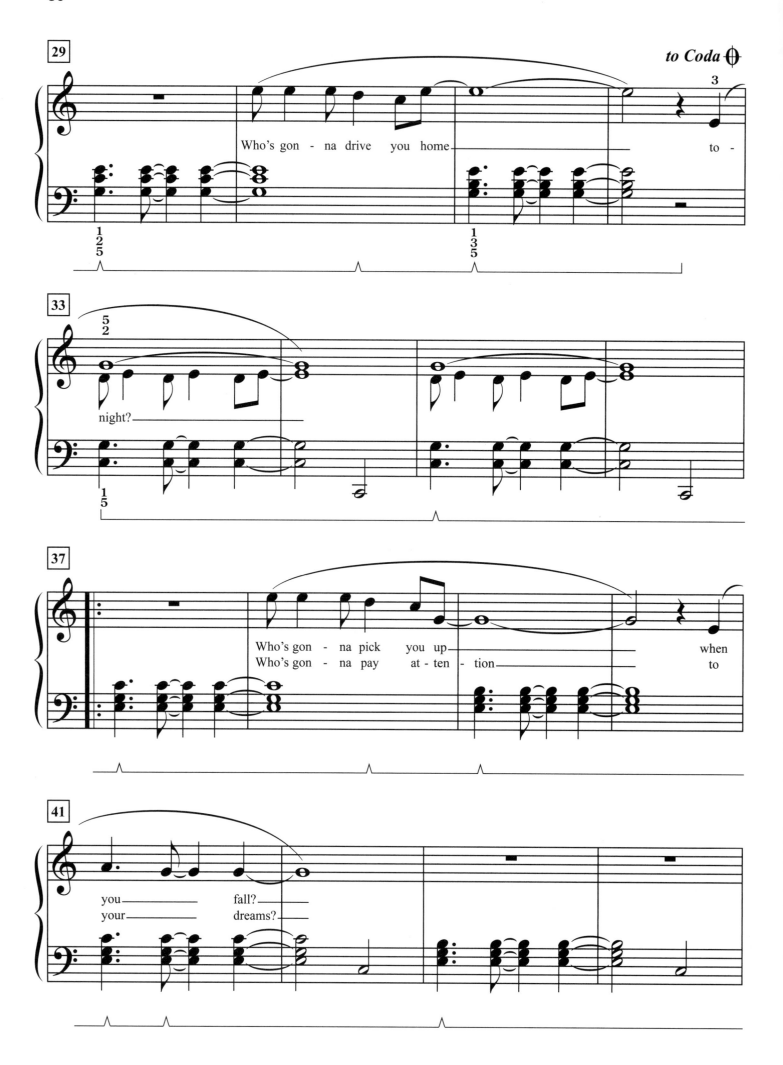

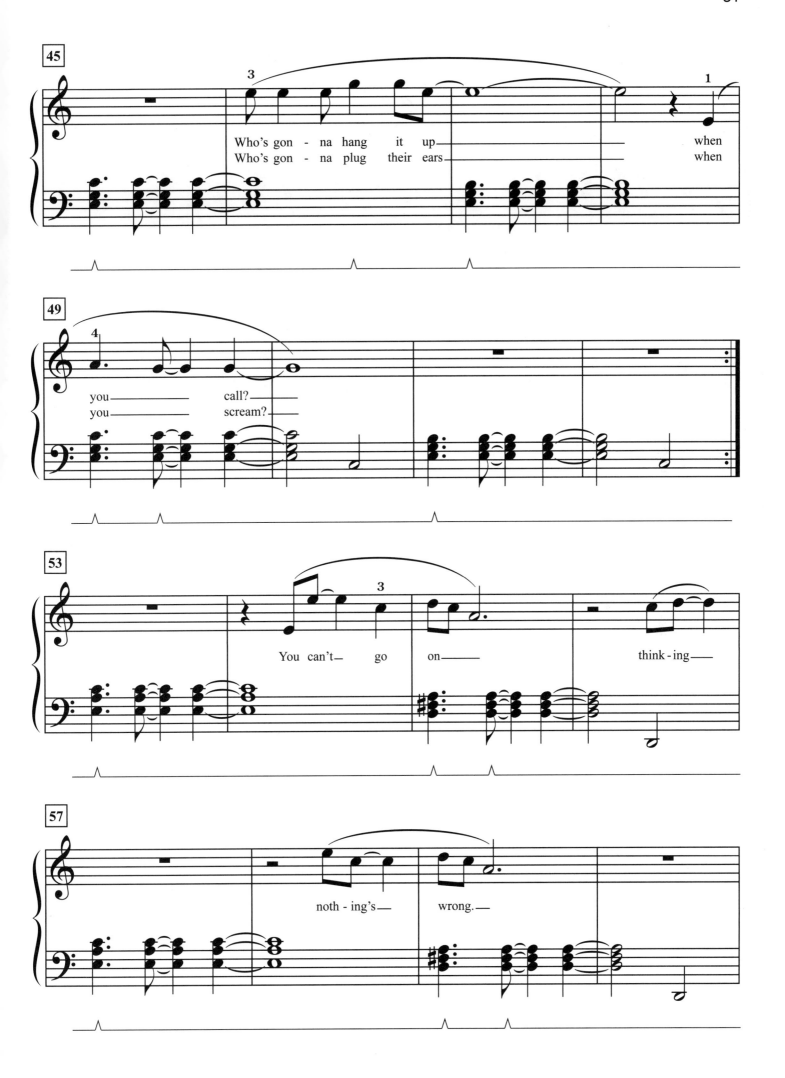

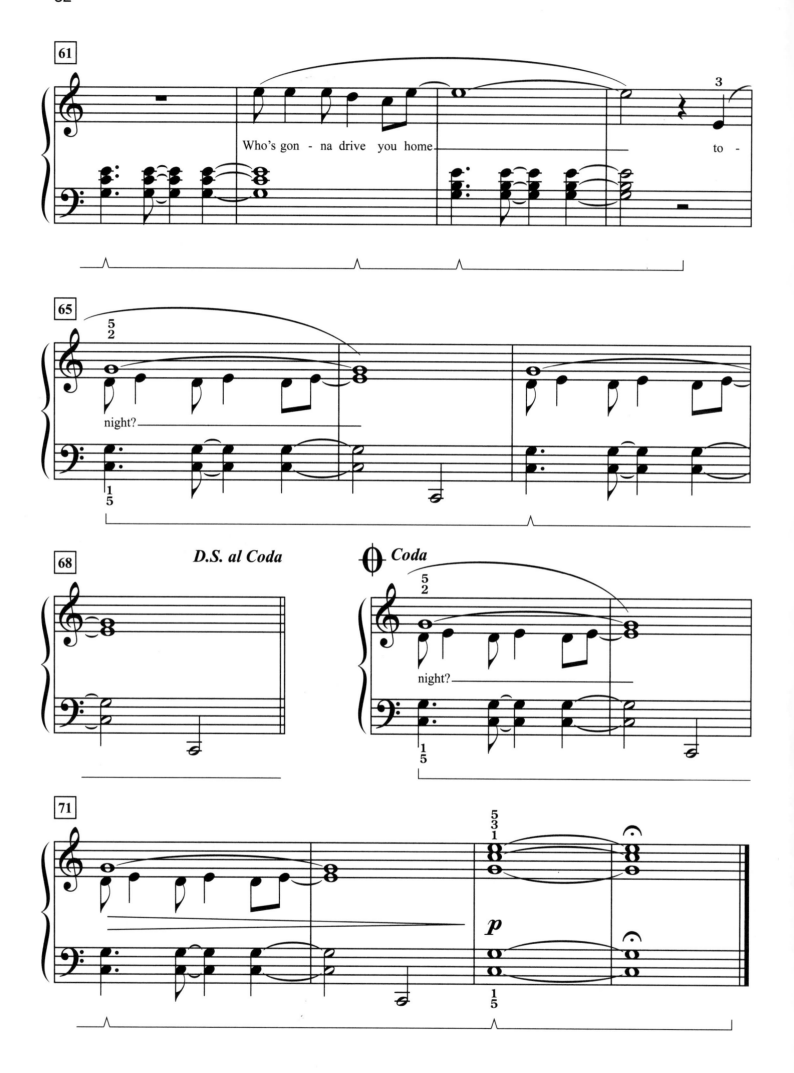

Higher Love

Words and Music by
Steve Winwood and Will Jennings
Arranged by Dan Coates

Moderate rock

Emotion in Motion

Words and Music by Ric Ocasek
Arranged by Dan Coates

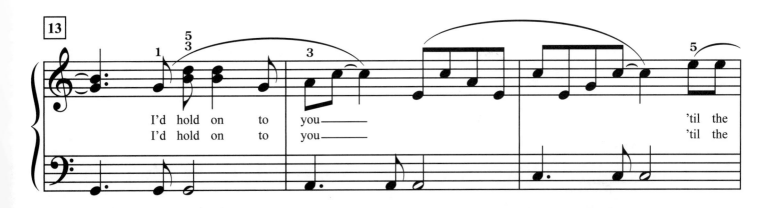

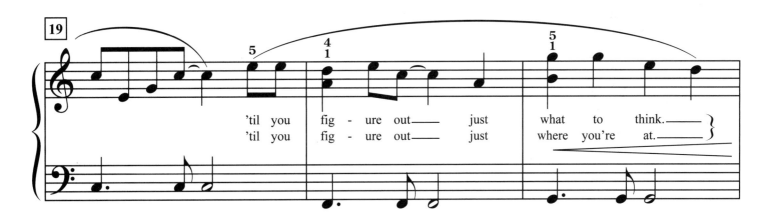

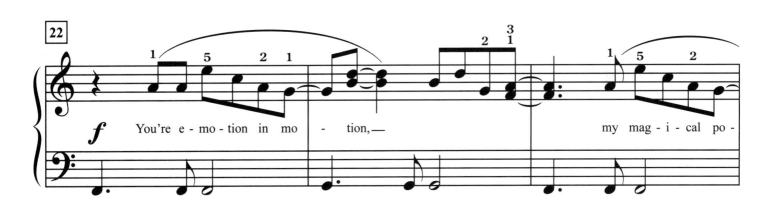

40

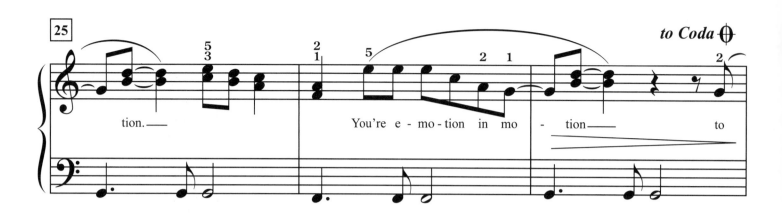

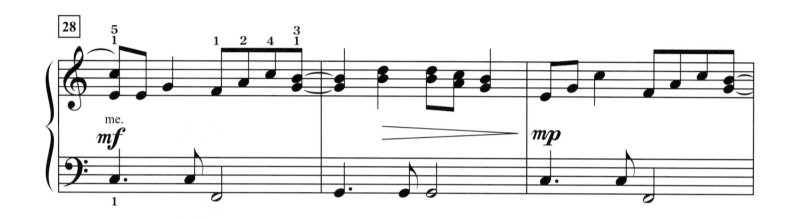

Eye of the Tiger

Words and Music by
Jim Peterik and Frankie Sullivan III
Arranged by Dan Coates

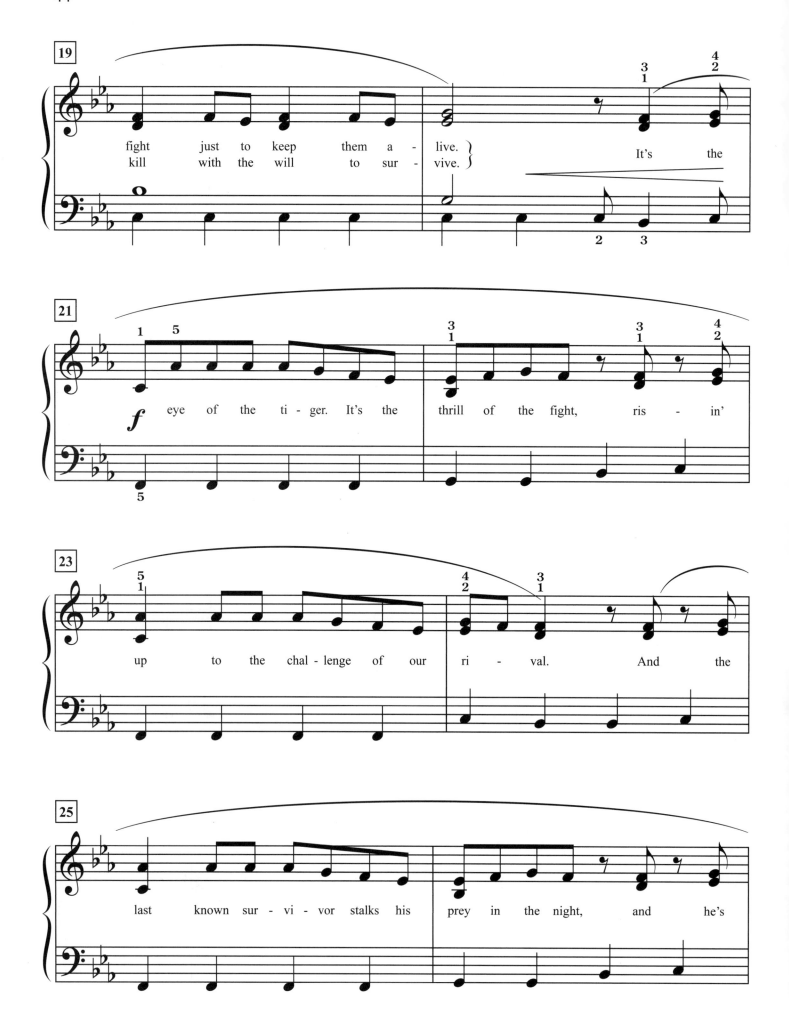

The Living Years

Words and Music by
Mike Rutherford and B. A. Robertson
Arranged by Dan Coates

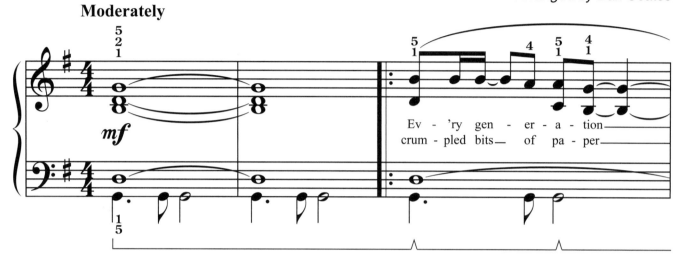

Is This Love

Words and Music by
Jim Peterik and Frankie Sullivan III
Arranged by Dan Coates

Moderate rock beat

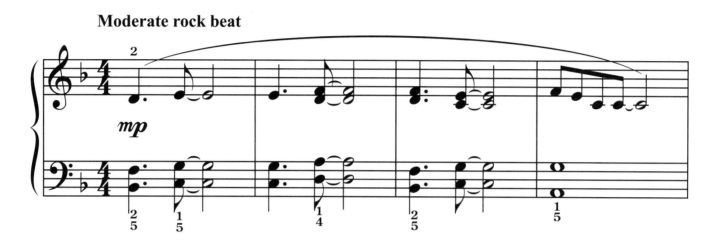

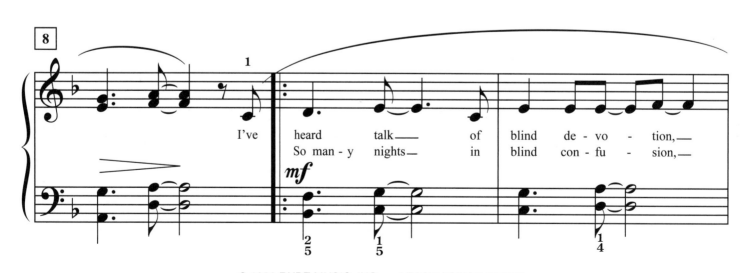

I've heard talk___ of blind de - vo - tion,___
So man - y nights___ in blind con - fu - sion,___

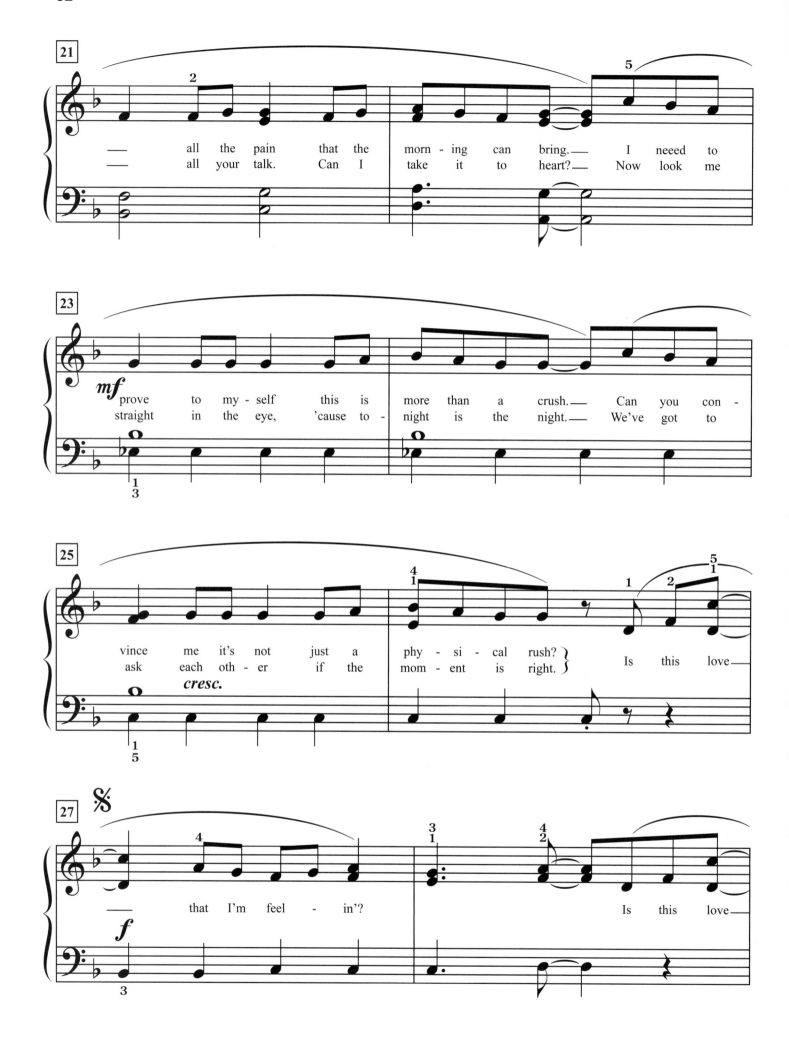

that's been keep-in' me up all night?— Is this love—— that I'm feel - in'?

to Coda ⊕ │1.

Is this love?—— *dim.*

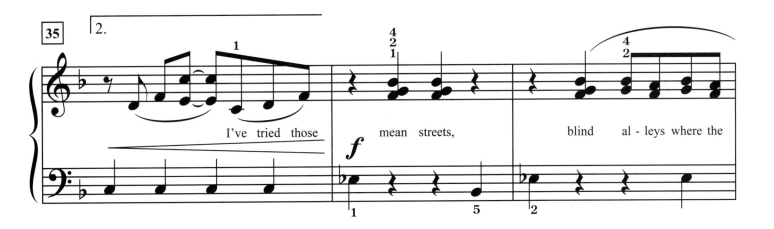

│2.

I've tried those mean streets, blind al - leys where the

f

cur - ren - cy of love chan - ges hands.—— All touch,

54

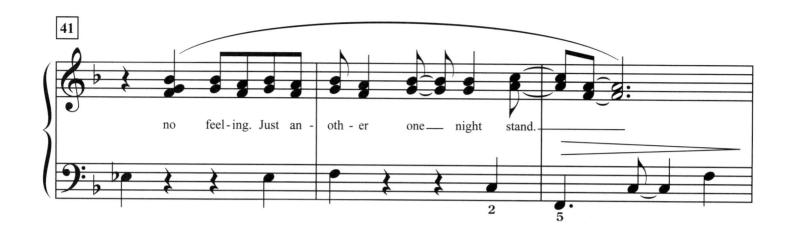

no feel-ing. Just an - oth - er one night stand.

I need to know that there's some-one who cares. Could you be the an - gel to

mf   cresc.

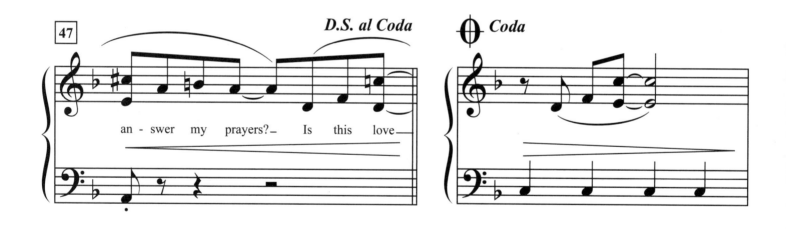

D.S. al Coda   Coda

an - swer my prayers? Is this love

mf   cresc.   sfz

You Belong to the City

Words and Music by
Glenn Frey and Jack Tempchin
Arranged by Dan Coates

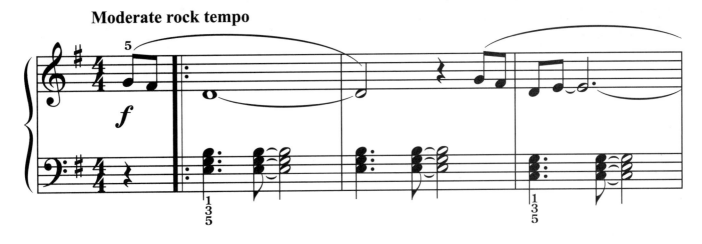

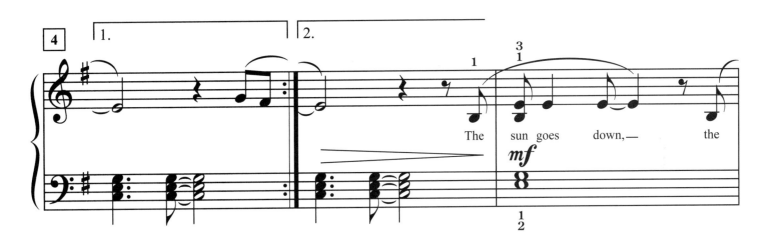

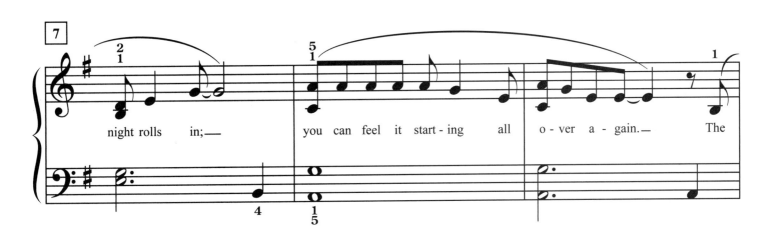

moon comes up—— and the mu - sic calls;— you're get - tin' tired of star - ing at the

same four walls. You're out of your room— and down on the street;—

mov - in' through the crowd and the mid - night heat;— the traf - fic roars,— the

si - rens scream,— you look at the fac - es, it's just like a dream.—

cresc.

No-bod-y knows— where you're go - in',— no-bod-y cares— where you've

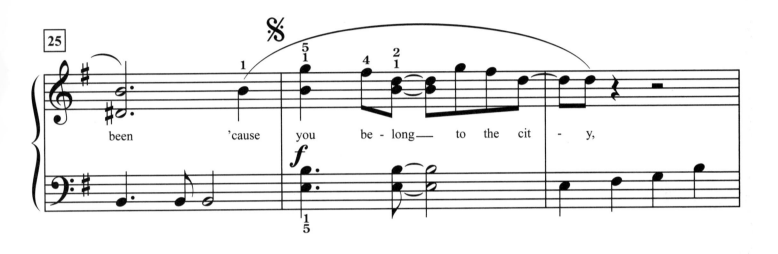

been 'cause you be - long— to the cit - y,

you be - long— to the night,— liv-in' in a riv-er of dark-

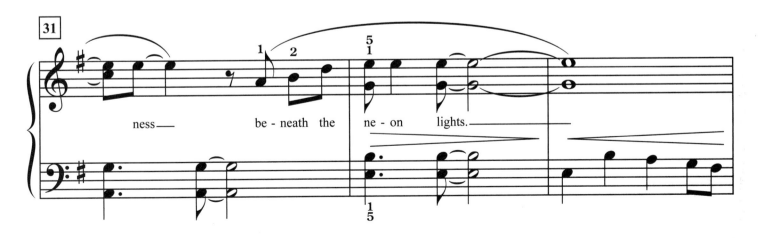

ness— be-neath the ne - on lights.—

46

back a - gain___ and you're feel - in' strange.___ So much has hap - pened, but

49

noth - ing has changed.___ You still don't know___ where you're go -

51 *D.S. al Coda*

in',___ you're still just a face___ in the crowd.

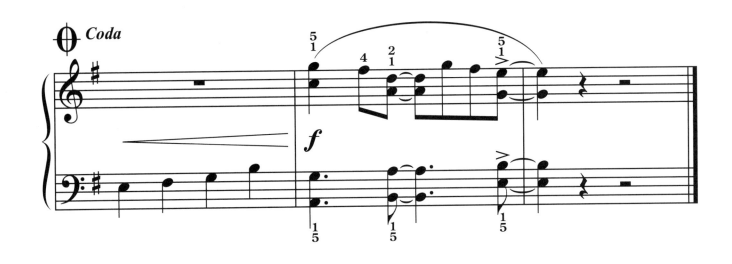

Coda

f

Open Arms

Words and Music by
Steve Perry and Jonathan Cain
Arranged by Dan Coates

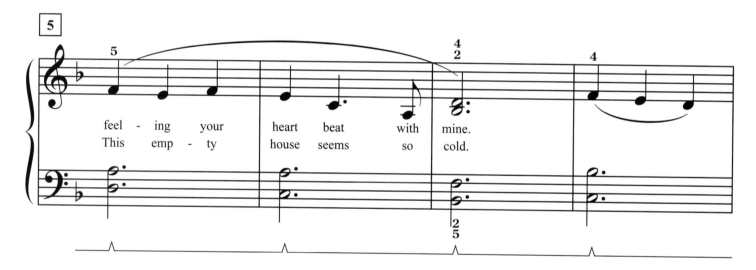

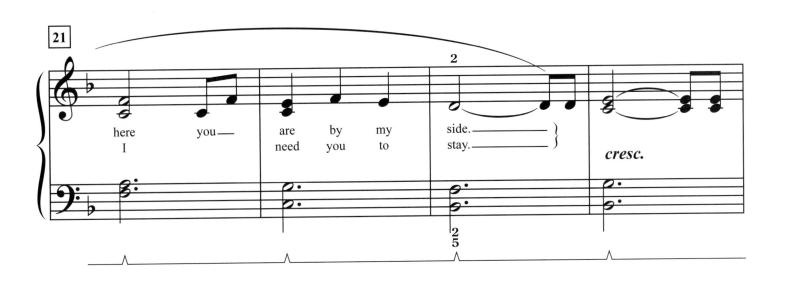

love means to   me;   o - pen arms.

Smuggler's Blues

Words and Music by
Glenn Frey and Jack Tempchin
Arranged by Dan Coates

Moderate rock beat

There's

trou - ble on the street to - night, I can feel it in my bones, — I
sail - ors and the pi - lots, the sol - diers and the law, — the

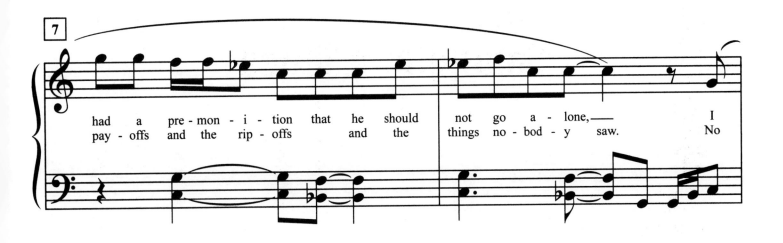

had a pre-mon-i-tion that he should / not go a-lone,— I
pay-offs and the rip-offs and the / things no-bod-y saw. No

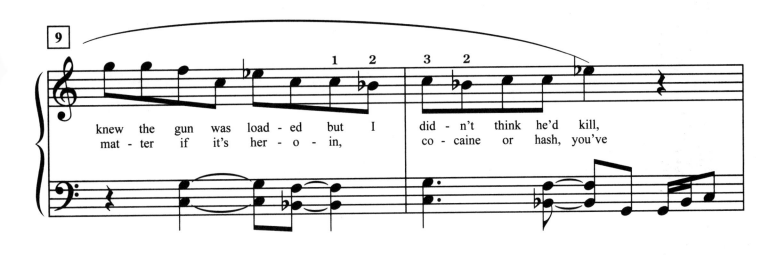

knew the gun was load-ed but I / did-n't think he'd kill,
mat-ter if it's her-o-in, / co-caine or hash, you've

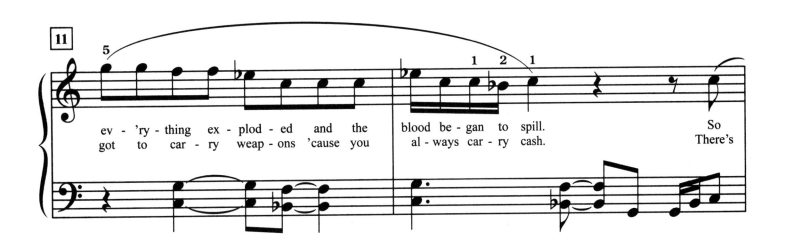

ev-'ry-thing ex-plod-ed and the / blood be-gan to spill. So
got to car-ry weap-ons 'cause you / al-ways car-ry cash. There's

Valerie

Words and Music by
Steve Winwood and Will Jennings
Arranged by Dan Coates

Steady rock beat

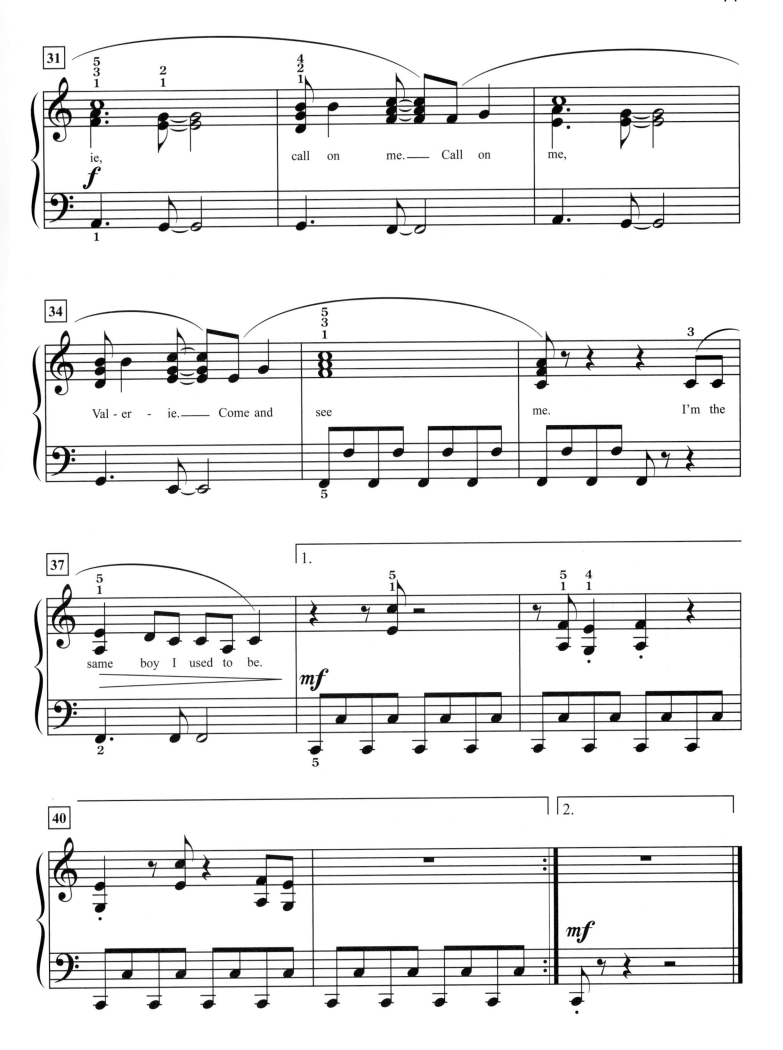

The Way You Make Me Feel

Written and Composed by Michael Jackson
Arranged by Dan Coates

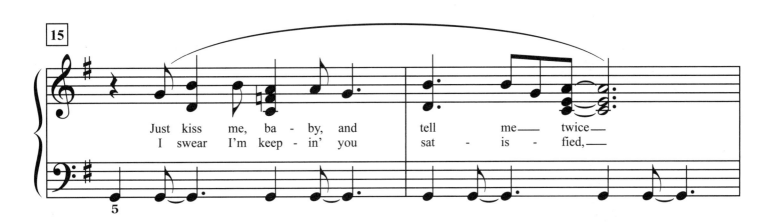

74

The way you make me feel, (The way you make me feel,

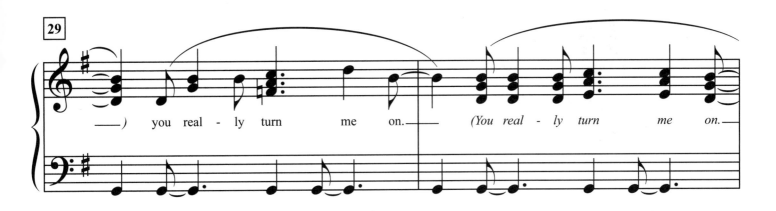

) you real-ly turn me on. (You real-ly turn me on.

) You knock me off of my feet. (You knock me off of my feet.

) My lone-ly days are gone! (My lone-ly days are gone!)

You Are the Girl

Words and Music by Ric Ocasek
Arranged by Dan Coates

Moderate rock beat

Why don't you dream an - y - more, —
Why don't we talk an - y - more, —

what's in the way?
what did I say?

How come you
How is it

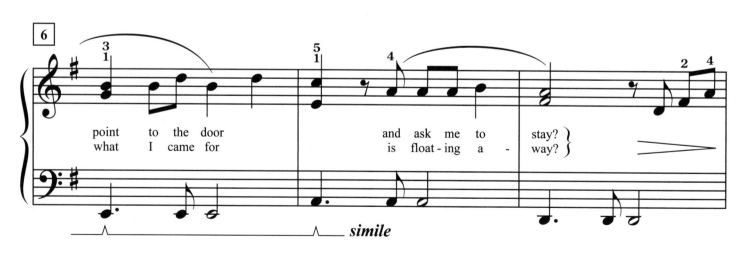

point to the door
what I came for

and ask me to stay?
is float - ing a - way?

simile

Alfred